The Protecto

by Chris Parker
Illustrated by Bill Ledger

OXFORD
UNIVERSITY PRESS

In this story ...

Evan
(Flex)

Evan has the power to stretch his body. He can reach all the way round the school!

Magnus
(caretaker)

Mr Trainer
(teacher)

Jin
(Swoop)

Magnus whistled as he swept the corridor.
He stopped suddenly as a strange, dark-haired
woman came towards him. She had some sort of
controller in her hand.

"Who are you?" Magnus asked.
The woman didn't reply. She just pointed the controller at Magnus and pressed a button. It made a buzzing noise.

"Hero Academy is mine," the woman said.
"Now, go outside."
Magnus turned and headed for the exit.

Meanwhile …

Mr Trainer was giving a lesson on villains. Jin nudged Evan. "I would rather be catching villains for real!" he whispered.

"You would never catch this villain," said Evan, showing Jin his tablet. "She can control people's minds and make them do what she wants."

Jin snorted. "No one can control *my* mind," he said.

"You can never be sure," Evan replied. "I've designed a new helmet to protect me. I call it ... the Protecto!"

Evan stretched his arm out of the classroom.

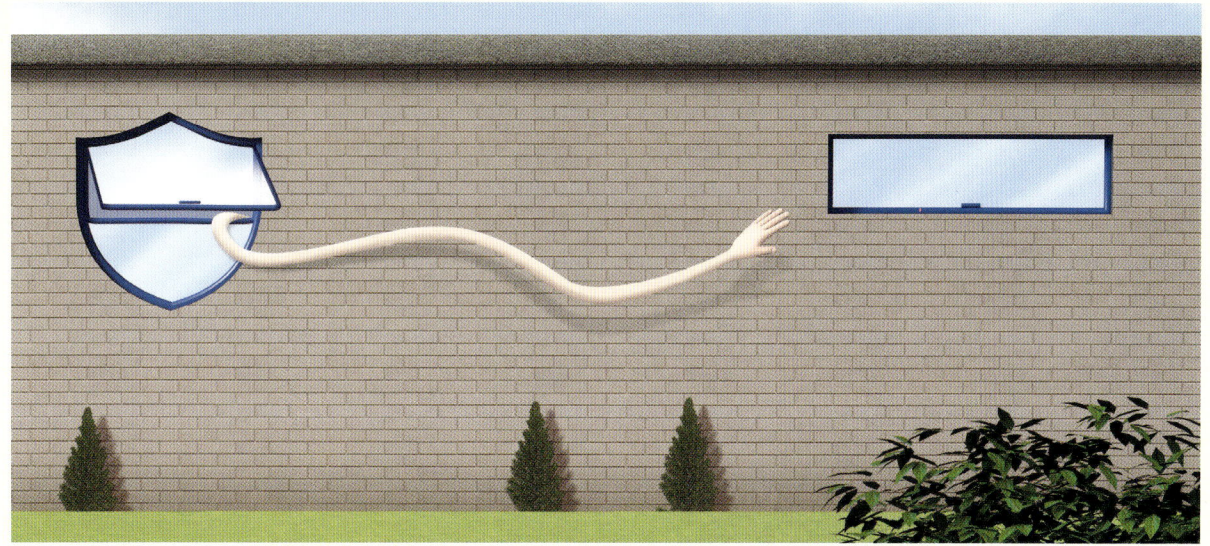

He reached into his locker and grabbed
the Protecto.

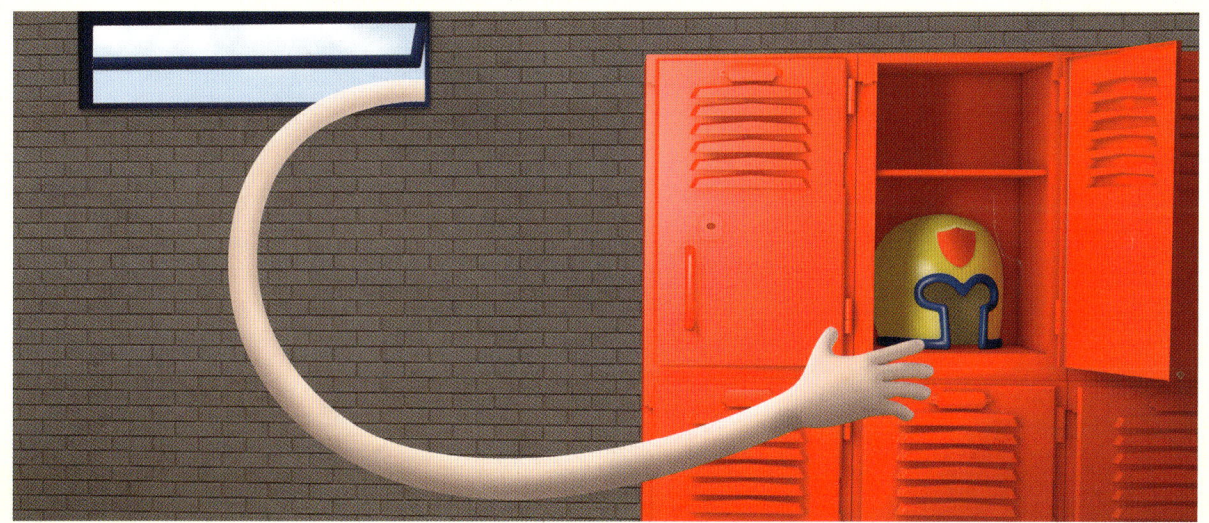

Evan put on the Protecto.

Jin giggled. "It looks a bit silly!"

Just then, a stranger came into the classroom.

Evan felt numb. "It's Doctor Daze!" he whispered.
Doctor Daze's controller made a buzzing noise.
A bright light shot out of it and hit Jin.

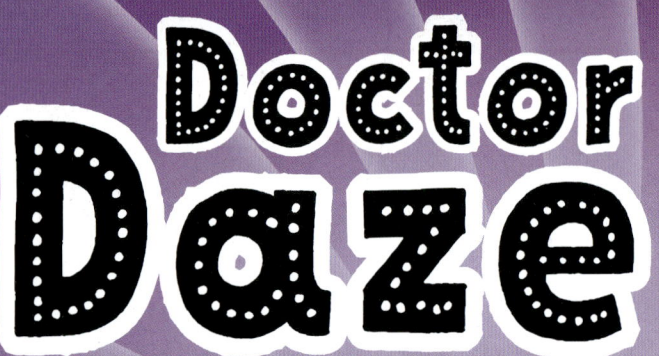
Doctor Daze

Catchphrase: I'll daze you for days!

Hobby: inventing gadgets.

Likes: people who do what she says, chocolate biscuits.

Dislikes: everyone else in the world!

Beware! Doctor Daze has made a number of gadgets that control people's minds. If you spot her, run the other way!

"Outside, right now!" ordered Doctor Daze.
"You! And you! Out!" she shouted, zapping
everyone in the room.
They all did as they were told.

Evan went out with the others. He pretended to be under Doctor Daze's control.
Doctor Daze stopped by the trophy cabinet.
"I love this cabinet!" she said. "My potted plant will look perfect here."

When they got outside, Doctor Daze shouted, "Listen to me! This is my house now. You will bring my furniture inside."

Evan knew he had to stop Doctor Daze. "I can't let her take over the academy!" he said.

Evan crept up behind Doctor Daze. He stretched out his arm. He was about to take the controller when Doctor Daze spun round. "Why aren't you helping the others?" she shouted.

Doctor Daze pressed the controller with her thumb, but the Protecto kept Evan safe. Evan snatched the controller from her. He lifted it up high so Doctor Daze could not reach.

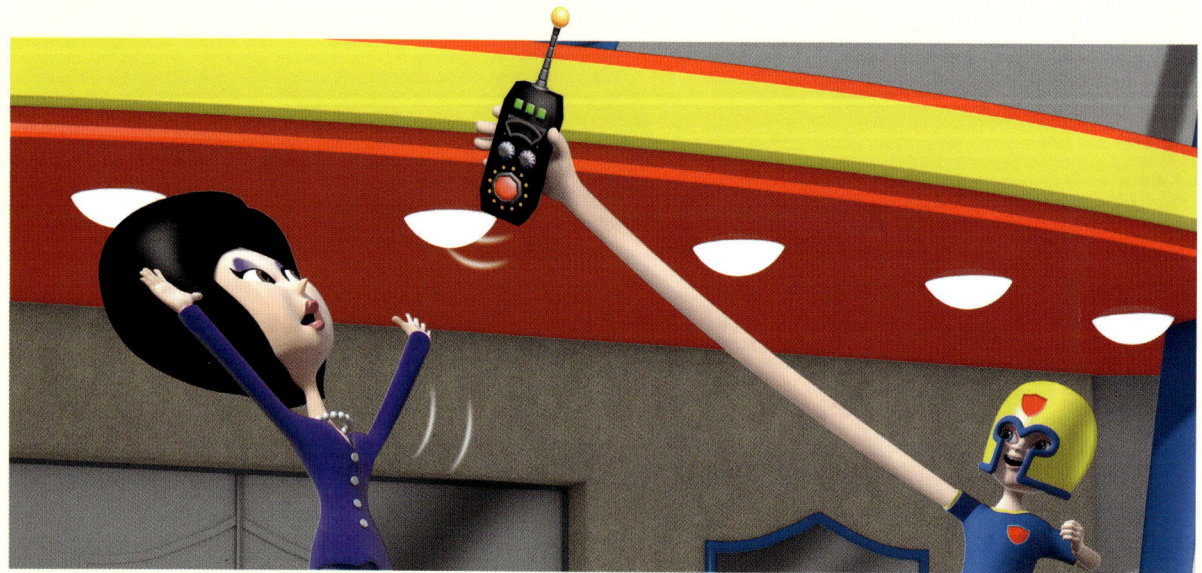

Doctor Daze turned ... and ran!

Evan pressed the reverse button on the controller.
One by one, everyone returned to normal.
They all cheered.

"Well done, Evan!" said Mr Trainer.
He took the controller and handed it to Magnus.
"Lock this somewhere safe please, Magnus,"
he said.

Just then, Evan saw a hover-bike zoom out of the van. "Doctor Daze is escaping!" he cried. "Don't worry," replied Mr Trainer. "Without her controller, she is not a danger to us."

"Er, Evan?" Jin said. "I was wrong. I don't think
the Protecto is silly after all. Can I have
one please?"
Evan smiled. "I think I'd better make one for
everyone!" he said.

Retell the story ...